OBSERVATIONS

1973 - 1986

Printed in the United States of America.

ISBN 978-0-9970242-3-4

J Winthrop, Charleston, South Carolina

www.winthropfamily.org

TO LIBBY

TABLE OF CONTENTS

Introduction

"Observations" is nothing more than a series of spontaneous ideas or thoughts committed to a pad of paper. They were written, for the most part, over a period of various challenges, a divorce, a battle for survival of a Wall Street firm, a struggle to provide a good home for sons amidst turmoil, and the creation of a new business enterprise.

These moments of peace and quiet along the way seemed worth recording, along with a little philosophy and the great joy my sons brought to my life.

These sketches were lost for a period of time and then rediscovered sometime after relocating in South Carolina.

J.W.
2006

OPEN AIR ASSIGNMENT

Children of the open air –
these three splendid young men –
looked at the cypress pond
and planned a canoe trip through it.

Children of the open air –
born into a competitive and complicated world –
forgot about school
as they launched a canoe and prepared a fire.

Collecting fallen branches in the piney woods,
these three splendid young men
created a barrier of stones
to contain a fire within a circle.

With warmth, fire, and smoke created,
the three woodsmen turned,
looked at the cypress pond
and prepared for the launching of the canoe.

A sapling anchored the silver canoe
by a rope from bow to branch.
With assignments clear the three boys slid off into the pond
and planned a canoe trip through it.

November 1973

DESTINY

Let's reach for the stars together
Let's stretch the limit
... and see what we can do.

Let's go for the big adventure
Let's take the chance
... and live the full life.

Let's explore the outer limits
Let's create our own future
... and make the game worthwhile.

For if we don't – if we don't take charge –
When we are able to do so –
Then the chance will be lost
To make this small planet
A better place
To live.

November 1973

BROTHERS

What a beautiful child our son Bayard is!
This dwarf-sized fellow with the golden locks.
This fellow who at 4½ says you made a mistake
when the conductor asks his age.
The big smile, the plea to come home
- or "to sleep with me" – or to "play with me"
- all of it will pass too quickly.

Bayard and Grenville fight terribly
but they also have some wonderful conversations
- about nature, about electric cars, pollution,
about the housing shortage and about large buildings.
They read together, too. Grenville can be very kind
in rare moments. As a child he was far more docile,
far more affectionate than most children his age.

November 1973

13

NO PLACE TO SWIM

There's something nearly ridiculous about the complaint
of not having a club swimming pool. I have heard it in
the affluent suburbs.

It is almost as if we don't remind ourselves of the
misfortune of others frequently enough. Half the world
is undernourished, a quarter of the world is starving,
and some of us are worrying about swimming pools.
The complaint often comes from the top 1% of our
population in terms of wealth – those with a net worth
of over a million and with annual incomes of over $100,000.

I guess my feeling is that it is OK to provide for a swim –
especially when the money has been earned through hard
work – but that there should be an offsetting and a mounting
concern for all those people who don't have food or shelter.
Because if we don't solve the larger problem there won't be
anyone around to worry about swimming pools anyway.

November 1973

HAPPY VISIT

What happiness it was to visit Adam

and his wife, and their little son,

on top of a high hill in Berkeley,

overlooking the twinkling lights of San Francisco!

We had dinner and talked.

Warmth radiated from their home –

their small apartment in the sky –

and the love they shared made the visitor forget

the world outside.

November 1973

ARIZONA MOUNTAIN SONG

Dry, vast land with big sky, big mountains
You dwarf man and make him see Truth.
The consequence of usual problems is placed in
proper focus.
Out here where a billion stars shine brighter than back home.

The sun-splashed mountainside cuts a vivid silhouette
Against the blue sky and offers peace to the weary traveler.
There is a beckoning, however faint, which says
"Come out here and learn to think as we do."

The mountains have endured so much
They offer a home for a thousand songbirds.

Spring 1974

MOVING ALONG

Open highway
inviting the lonely traveler
to explore the rolling landscape,
brings a new experience.

The active mind turns off
the passive mind turns on
absorbing the hills and the cars
the flowers and the speedometer
the trees and the fuel gauge.

All the beauties of nature
seen between blinks
on the open highway
What a pity
that we cannot slow down.

July 1974

A POEM A DAY

If we could only write
A poem every day ...
It might help avoid the strife
And bring pleasure into life.

It would keep us on our toes
Whether poetry or prose.

It would make us look around
And absorb what can be found.

If we could only write
A little every day ...
We could fill the idle hours
And make sunshine out of showers.

We could freeze those good impressions
And avoid the lonely sessions.

We could make music out of words
And imitate the birds.

If we could only write ...

March 1975

GREENERY

The mist hung over the meadows in the early morning
As we climbed into our canoes and cast out into the river
The swirls and eddies preoccupied us at first
As we paddled around them to keep our craft afloat.

But then we could drift with the mighty Delaware
And look at the world float by along the riverbank
The overwhelming impression was one of peacefulness
Of bursting spring buds and of greenery.

The trees in May sport their freshest coat of green
The fields and grass roll as a green blanket along the bank
The splashes of sun and a tableau of various shades
Offer a balm to the spirit after the mist burns off.

May 1975

CULINARY DELIGHT

Having been appointed chef
For a group of fathers and sons on a camping trip
I sorted out my limited wares –
A pan, a boiler, a fork, some soup, some bacon,
Some plates.

A city-bred, briefcase-carrying,
Out-of-shape, over-dressed,
Out-of-his-element father
Cooking for a group of campers.

The fire was built
The soup went on; the bacon went on.
A stir here; and an adjustment there
As confidence began to build.

A crowd of hungry boys gather about
Awaiting the long-delayed meal
Some pepper here, some salt there
As satisfaction grew.

A log slipped; the grill slid
Soup and bacon began to walk away
Mercifully both were stopped and served to all our pals.

June 1975

ARE YOU SAD?

I went to his room
To say prayers
To talk
And to kiss my child.

He had developed lumps
All over his body – bug bites
And his nose was running
He had been uncomfortable.

I sat on his bed
And not a moment had passed
When he looked at me and said
"Are you sad?"

He reached out and patted my hand
"How could I ever be sad for long
When I have three such fine young men?"
I told him that. (What a splendid fellow!)

June 1975

ONE-EYED BALLPLAYER

The seven- and eight-year-olds assembled for the game
Big boys, small boys ... some girls
And one fellow with a glass eye.

The game began – a kaleidoscope of incompetence
Walks and errors and very little action
Until the little boy half-blind stepped up to bat.

The bases were filled – all walked batters
The parents were interested in the children
    – bored with the game.
But the drama of the moment swept through the crowd.

This gentle child with a missing eye
Measured the incoming pitch and swung his bat
Driving the ball through the infield and
Into right field.

Everyone cheered and this extraordinary boy was very,
    very happy.

June 1975

WICKED BIKE

The eldest son
Tough to let him know
How proud you are
Of his leadership
Of his intelligence
Of his good sense

… Especially when he
Does not want Dad's
Praise and does want
A motorcycle … so badly.

What a great boy!
He deserves more than
"a wicked bike"

August 1975

MORNING VISIT

Simple fun it was ...
Driving to our coastal hideaway
And walking down through the long grass
To the beach.

Grenville, now nine and sturdy
Was a good companion
On this morning away from camp
With his dad.

Nature's creatures still held his interest –
The saucy loon drifting offshore
The "shrimp" bug – jumping vertically
The helpless crabs and muscles and starfish.

What fun it was
To communicate by the water's edge
And take a swim and then have lunch
It made me said to leave him back at camp.

August 1975

24

ODE TO MIRNA

You keep things tidy in an untidy world.
You make children happy when they might well
    have been sad.
You grow flowers in barren soil
And you spread good cheer in your quiet way.

Your grace and poetry
Your gentleness and flowers
Your kindness and beauty
Will be with us forever.

I will always be grateful
… for all of this.
I will remember all the times
… you helped us all.

We miss you so very much!

September 1975

WORKAHOLIC

Up early
Get on the train
After washing ... after dressing ... after driving
Get off train
Get on subway
Walk

Arrive at work
Action begins
Enjoyable ... painful ... interesting ... boring
Unpredictable action
Meetings ... phone calls ... letters ... memos
No rest

Lunch break
Think, rest, eat, rest, think, go

More meetings, more mail, more problems, more crises
The day wears on
Oblivious to the clock at times; strapped to the clock
At times
And so the day goes.

August 1975

FRANK

A man of grace and kindness
Who teaches people that black is good
We owe him so much.

Big frame, narrow waist,
Open face, wonderful smile,
Totally black.

Man of the Carolina earth
Warm and gentle as a southern breeze.
We would like to know and understand you better.
We would like you to break bread with us
And communicate
We would like to learn more about your ways.

But who gives a damn what we would like.
It is better this way.
One cannot pick a forest flower and carry it home.

August 1975

MY THREE SONS

Bayard asleep –
Tousled and plump
Snoring and sunburned
Peaceful, oblivious, adorable.
I will always be near you in my thoughts
And all too rarely in fact.

March 1976

Grenville ...
Enigmatic and complex
Passionate and pugilistic
Sensitive, modest, beautiful.
Please call me if you need me
And never forget your Dad loves you.

March
1976

John, Jr., firstborn
Bright and competitive
Intense and involved
Careful, optimistic, loyal.
You and your hardy brothers
Bring me such joy!

March
1976

GROWING OLDER

Grenville, the second boy, is growing older. He has begun to stretch out, to make sense, to apply himself, to show good judgment. The blossoming is often hidden but was strongly evident when he wanted to sit down and talk with me in our living room in South Carolina – the Big House where people of all ages come together and communicate – a special place which evokes the need in all of us to reach out. He asked about the trees, about the future ...

I read him my thoughts on the tree farm for the year 2000. I explained that we needed to think about timber volume, about our approach to farming, even housing capacity on the property as well as wildlife and animals. Then I read him the management objective.

He liked it.

April 1976

A VISIT WITH FRANCES WHITE

Somehow in that hot and noisy living room I knew that something very unusual was happening. A lady who was nearly blind, very black, and now old was telling me she felt blessed and very fortunate to have worked for such good people as my family. As the jackhammers and tractors dug a sewer, she had me read a document dedicated some time ago to her granddaughter. It was handwritten. The six-page description of her life, her service to the Winthrop family, and her impression of earlier days in Estill and on Groton Plantation emphasized only the bright and positive aspects and totally bypassed the hardships she obviously has suffered.

As she embellished the story here and there, she smiled and radiated a convincing happiness. The room was terribly hot. The document described her few trips away from the area in rich detail. The trips were mostly for medical reasons. No mention was made of the difficulties experienced in going blind. I asked her about her life now. No complaints. She had her health and her mind worked well. No mention of God, although I knew she was deeply spiritual. She had almost no hair; she was thinner now than she had been. Yet she appeared very strong and at peace as we sat in her living room on that steamy day.

I noticed my Christmas card to her was framed – a picture of my three boys – and sitting on the table amongst the pictures of members of her own family. When I commented on all her pictures, she had a child sitting quietly beside her bring from her bedroom two new pictures – one of her grandmother and one of her grandfather – both very well dressed and handsome people. They had just been sent to her. Her grandparents had lived in slavery times, she said.

Before leaving, I was able to tell her how much she had brought to so many people's lives. I asked her how old she was. "Eighty-one," she said, "born in 1888." It was August, 1979.

A TRIP HOME

Johnny Earl Williams, carpenter, all around laborer, farmer, black man, friend always, was shuffling home from work one evening. I stopped my car to give him a ride. The late afternoon sun was still unbearably hot. As we drove along the sandy road dust flew high in the air, chickens and dogs cleared a way for us as we drove by a neighbor's house. Within a few minutes my aging black friend was arriving home with me. Usually Johnny walked home; today he had a driver.

Johnny's granddaughter awaited us – speechless but obviously excited by the sight of my passenger. I offered her a ride but she declined, preferring the familiarity and warmth this fine man offered her. "Hi Sugar," he said, and put his big arm around her. Together they walked back to their cabin after he thanked me. It was odd. I felt very emotional as I drove away – deeply moved by the sight of my friend with a child he loved.

August 1979

FISHING TRIP

It was a tropical, heavy southern day – too hot to move, too
hot to walk, too hot to go fishing. I picked the time to ask
my third son to walk a mile with me to fish in a pond.
He complained bitterly, but finally joined me. There was
very little else to do that day and we all-too-rarely did
things together. I wish I did more with all my boys.

We walked endlessly along the sandy road on the way to
the Ivanhoe Pond. After a while the trees almost seemed to
dance in the heat; the bugs were always out of swatting
distance and fiendishly intense. The pine cones and flowers
required too much effort to pick up even though we had
containers for them. We pressed on – beads of sweat
forming streams and then rivers on our faces.

Presently we came upon a slight rise in the land and gazed
upon the expanse of water ahead of us. The very sight of
it almost offered relief from the heat. The world changed.
We moved toward it. Bayard stopped complaining,
brightened and prepared to fish as we approached
the water. We talked about airplanes, our cabin, fish, and
things we enjoyed. It was a rare encounter despite the
heat and maybe more memorable because of it.

August 1979

VACATION THOUGHTS

August, 1979, was devoted to vacationing with all three boys – possibly the last chance for a total vacation together in this way. It was well worth the cost. We had a few difficult times but all in all it was a splendid success.

In returning, I face the mysteries of John, Jr.'s future in boarding school, uncertainties of court battles involving children and money, and finally, the endless challenges of the office. But there is no doubt that time away from the daily cares restores perspective. In addition to allowing all three boys the chance to be together, this month offered me the opportunity to ...

- think sensibly about my will and estate matters
- plan for the balance of this year away from the office
- develop more in the way of a five-year plan for my land

On a more practical level I was able to ...

- clean up litter on my land and prepare for more trees on Ivanhoe and Seminole
- appear on television in two cities and help educate more than 100,000 South Carolinians about mutual funds
- send off 50 appeals for The Fresh Air Fund
- plan for a swimming pool in Allendale as the next project for the Family Foundation (STW)
- draft two literary efforts along with annual notes for Ivanhoe
- improve banking and legal ties in the area along more tangible lines
- establish a relationship with our hunting club on Ivanhoe and stress conservation, litter prevention, and our mutual responsibilities (all of this at a picnic attended by 15 members and a local politician)

More could be added to these lists. While the boys hunted and fished, I dreamed and worked. It was a very different kind of month for all of us.

September 1979

ON LOVE

My opinion of love changes with each passing day. It is a
word one must not use too frequently or carelessly. The word
has been misunderstood, abused, and treated carelessly.
Love has created pain and anguish, tears and isolation.

All of this is too bad because at all times and every day
of our lives love must be considered an elevating experience
– a relationship in spiritual greatness. It is generous and
joyful in the giving; it is nourishing and enhancing in the
receiving. Love does not involve any form of possessing
or dominating. Rather in love we affirm and strengthen one
another. In its purest form for me love is unconditional –
allowing freedom and joy.

October 1979

ON GOOD LUCK

How lucky we are to be alive at this time and in this place!
To be a citizen of the most exciting and prosperous major
country on earth as we approach the 1980s is worth a
moment of thought and a good dose of appreciation.
Democracy and capitalism continue to work long after
many had predicted the demise of both. The gifts of modern
science and medicine have enriched and prolonged our lives.

How lucky we are also to have been born into a family
of means and with a sense of identity. It is important to
understand that this dimension is pure accident of birth
and that we simply stand on the shoulders of those who
have gone before us as a nation and as a family.

If we are among the luckiest in America, and we surely are,
we are clearly among the luckiest on earth!

This is a little sermon I preach to myself regularly. It seems
a good idea to repeat it in a poor country.

October 1979

CHILDREN – EARLY THOUGHTS

Before we know it they are grown up and gone.
How many generations of parents have said the same thing?
The poignancy of it all almost brings on tears. And yet, when
we think about it, we know that life's journey is but a moment
in the clock of time, and if there is any such thing as a grand
design we know we are but instruments of God's will in the
perpetuation of the species.

Our children share the voyage with us. They improve the trip,
I think. Before long they will think they know better ways of
doing things than we do. They tolerate our old fashioned
ways and then choose their own course. It would all be very
distressing to me if I didn't pause a moment and realize that I
behaved the same way myself. Still, it's sad to see the little
birds leave the nest – barely before they have learned to fly.

October 1979

ON MAKING MONEY

It is sad that the pursuit of gold can be so consuming for individuals worthy of so much more. Down deep it is the quest for security that drives us. Uncertain in a world which threatens our future too many are channeled by the urge to make more money – too often driven by greed and insecurity.

I feel certain the day will come that we will all learn that we could have operated on a higher level; that we could have been charged with nobler ambition ... if only we could see the larger picture ... understand the grand design.
We were not put on this planet to add to our riches.
More was expected of us. I'm sure of that.

December 1979

ON GROTON MEADOW

To me our home in Greenwich has always been beautiful,
and yet I have not always been entirely comfortable in
the community. While the town of Greenwich and life
in Greenwich has always run against the grain with me,
in some way difficult to explain how, the yellow house with
the black shutters in the back country has always been
a comfortable retreat.

The meadow itself seems to change with as much regularity
as the ocean. The pure snows of winter melt into the warm
winds of April. The flowers dance and change into the spring
and summer while the cutting of the grass always brings
swallows, crows, and songbirds. In the fall the autumn
colors blend into the scene and change it once again.

This has been my home for a long, long time,
but I doubt it will remain so forever.

January 1980

ON IMPULSE

Rather than establish a list of categories and subjects
for these short musings, it seems wiser to act on impulse.
Allowing one subject to flow into another seems
a little better and a little easier.

An athlete cannot be given too much structure once the
basic sport is learned. A pitcher in baseball will not always
throw a strike, but his flow of motion may carry him the full
nine innings and maybe even win the game.

I will continue my compulsive note-taking because it
seems to be a part of my natural flow of energy. There
will be no game to win and no clearly defined purpose.
I simply have to do it on impulse.

January 1981

ON HATRED

Hatred is such a useless, unproductive emotion. It derails us from the daily journey of life and consumes our emotions and energy. Upon occasion I have found it useful to simply let time pass when individuals or even groups of people develop negative feelings toward one another. In this way only is it possible to examine the roots of the disease.

Feelings of inadequacy, feelings of isolation, or feelings of insecurity can come into focus and be understood better when time passes. Then, when communication begins, the sickness might be cured gradually. This basic truth, it seems to me, can prevail among nations as well as among individuals.

March 1981

ON NEW ENGLAND

When it comes to where my home is, there is no question about it. My social and spiritual roots are firmly planted in New England soil. It is where I was born; it is where I was educated; it is where I consider home.

These thoughts came to me while in Botswana. Perhaps they were planted by a water bird, which sounded like a seagull. Seagulls used to fly over our home on the North Shore of Massachusetts.

June 1981

ON THE COAST

In like manner, I have a strong sense of belonging to the edge of the New England coastline. The crowing of Singing Beach in Massachusetts has broadened my thirst for the more remote areas of the Maine coast or further north along the coast of Canada.

But in my mind's eye, I can often see the strong waves crashing against the beaches and rocky coastline of New England. My ears can still hear the song of the gulls and the doleful blast of the distant foghorn. I can even smell the salt air. Oceanfront fantasies are always rich for me.

September 1981

ON THE WOODS

The piney forests of South Carolina, as well, have given us renewed energy since childhood. Maybe it is their vibrant green. Firmly planted in the sandy soil and red clay earth of the Low Country, they provide their own brand of peace for the weary traveler while giving shelter to wildlife and beauty to the landscape. The South, too, is part of our life.

For every one of the full-grown slash or loblolly or long-leaf pine trees we cut, we must plant two so that our children and grandchildren can share the peace and joy of the forest.

January 1982

ON IVANHOE POND

If there is one location in the entire world that has made time stop for me, it is the Ivanhoe Pond. I cannot say whether it is the abundance of wildlife – ducks, deer, quail, turkeys, raccoons, otters, and all the species of that have surrounded it and come to it. I cannot say if it is the cabin we have had built by its shores, which allows us a constantly changing view of this brand of wilderness.

It may even be that my busy life has allowed so little time to really enjoy the Ivanhoe Pond that I dream about it too much and long for its serenity.

Somehow I doubt it. Ivanhoe Plantation has been a rewarding lifetime enterprise, and the Ivanhoe Pond is the crowning jewel of that property.

May 1982

ON GROTON PLANTATION

Groton Plantation has been a great luxury for three generations of our family, but it is beginning to become more of a source of pain than joy. Access to the place has become more restricted with growing numbers of owners and family members. The business problems of managing the property seem to have multiplied as the challenges of farming, growing trees, and hunting have mounted. Most of all, the complicated problems of estate planning make the preferences among family members for ownership and "club membership" rise to the surface and resentments are beginning to form. We need to gift this magnificent piece of land to the next generation and put an easement on it so that parts of it cannot be lost and the next generation can enjoy it.

With all the aforementioned reasons, an owner who feels insecure or is driven by the need to preach or threaten his brothers or cousins will drive a poison which will be hard to remove into the system. Maybe wisdom will prevail on Groton Plantation, but I think now I prefer Ivanhoe, which is smaller and less dramatic, but free from the complications.

October 1982

ON TESSIE

Any group of miniature essays constructed by me upon reaching the age of fifty would be incomplete without a word about my dog, Tessie – my pet, my best friend and even my confidant in years past.

She was a lovely half-breed mutt – a cross between a Labrador and an English Setter, but looking more like the Setter. The first two years of her life she was fed and walked by me in the confines of New York City. But when she was carried down to Groton Plantation she was clearly happier romping across the fields and forests in search of quail and birds, or curled up on my bed at night.

Tessie was housebroken, obedient – far more intelligent than most dogs – and intensely loyal to me. Even though no more than a month of each year was spent by our family on our place in South Carolina, she would always leap with excitement as I approached her in the kennels, where she spent most of the remaining eleven years.

The intensity of my joy upon arrival or my despair upon our departure from Groton has remained unmatched to this day – largely because of Tessie.

When she was put to sleep I was away in the Navy. I tried to comfort myself with the thought that she was at peace in death. But what a loss it was!

March 1983

ON MOTHER

Speaking of loyalty (a quality I value highly), my mother
always stuck with me, doted on me, laughed with me, and
seemed to take pride in me throughout our time together.

Mummy's frailties and faults were up front and obvious to
me since I was six years old:

- She drank too much and smoked too much
- She gossiped too much and she was too social
- She practiced favoritism and was not always sensitive with
  those who had problems

But ...

- She was brave in facing adversity
- She was simplistic, but clear in her philosophy
- She had a wonderful sense of humor

Most of all, she valued Harvard, aristocracy and
tradition. She was inspired by great music and
the Episcopalian church.

Finally, she nurtured the unrealistic thought that her
eldest son was capable of doing almost anything.

What an unusual mixture of qualities!
What an unforgettable character!

January 1984

ON FATHER

More remote, more confusing, and far more democratic was my father. He was a man of means who carried his own bags; he was a man who loved the city, who loved to grow trees and ride in the country; he was a man who was a model of good manners and yet tolerated all kinds of non-conforming behavior; he was a man who belonged to fancy clubs but wore red socks while playing tennis on the most proper courts.

Daddy was a man who took traveling more seriously than his work, who took giving more seriously than getting, and who took Democrats far more seriously than Republicans.

All of these contradictions left his eight children a little bewildered at times, but in our bones we knew that we had a thoroughly decent man as our father.

February 1984

ON CHILDREN

The people most judgmental about how to rear children
are those who haven't had any.

The beauty of having children is that it forces any intelligent
adult to consider deeply the needs of others.

The process of seeing children grow and develop is more
than just satisfying to some. It is what makes a large part
of life worthwhile.

The control of any parent over the actual long-term behavior
of any child is very, very limited. One can only hope that by
steering them in the right direction that all will be well and the
better genes will govern. As a wise man said many years
ago, the arrow can be aimed into the sky but its path and
eventual landing place cannot be governed.

As children become adults, one can only be thankful that
each has survived the many opportunities for danger and
disaster in the early years.

November 1984

ON IRREVERENCE

A footnote on being contrary-minded occurred to me this morning as I read the newspaper ...

Just because we are told something is true, we must not accept it – but rather verify it for ourselves. Just because we read something in an authoritative newspaper or magazine, it is important to try to verify it on our own.

Even when we develop a high level of respect for some older and possibly wiser person, it is important to find our own way and to do what "feels right" or is verifiable in our own ball park.

It is difficult to remember the above all of the time, but it is worth reminding myself of it, I feel.

February 1985

ON ART

It is curious how some works of art grow in beauty over time and others seem to fade away. An uncle who collected art used to say he wouldn't purchase a painting unless "it sang to him."

The unseasoned eye, my own included, cannot always identify the works of art that "sing." However, with the passing of time the discrimination process has improved for me, and, as for the Great Masters, there is no doubt that such well-known artists as Constable, Ingress, and Turner are among my favorites. Their masterpieces "sing" to me.

Perhaps we need to spend a little more time in the galleries.

March 1985

ON MUSIC

One of God's greatest gifts to man has been that of
granting him the ability to create music. Music is to the
ear what spices are to the sense of taste, what flowers
are to the sense of smell, and what wonders of nature
are to the sense of sight.

Think of the splendid symphonies of Beethoven – perhaps
his greatest – created when he was nearly totally deaf.
What a gift to humanity!

The universality of great music – just as great literature or
great art – has provided inspiration and joy to mankind for
centuries. And the less great music, while it may not survive
as long, gives each generation a new beat, a new tune, and
a new melody. Music can add enormous richness to life …
at least to my life.

January 1986

ON GULPING

Trying to prove he had a great zest for life, a foolish fellow
once said he was a gulper and not a sipper.

One could only envision him with all four feet in the trough
slurping up whatever was to be drunk and then lurching away
without even wiping the drool from his beard.

Given a choice, however, I would rather commit to a total
experience in life rather than tiptoe around the edges.
Maybe I, too, am a gulper, with all it implies.

Sipping is not my style, but if I am a gulper,
I will try to remember my manners.

February 1986

ON REAL ESTATE

Having one's own turf is important. In my world of
dreams, the real estate I want to own and share with
my family lies on the coast with the waves crashing
in from the open sea. At other times it is a patch of
woods where I may wander in peace.

Urban real estate has no psychic value for me.
Who cares about owning a piece of a mall or a shopping
center or a skyscraper! The investment may be rewarding,
but it's always better to get the psychic dividends as well
as the tangible ones.

In the final analysis, we own nothing anyway. We come
into this world with nothing and we leave it with nothing.
But if we have an opportunity to own – or more
accurately – to be a trustee of a piece of land, to improve
it or to safeguard its environmental integrity, then we have
done something of consequence.

March 1986

ON WRITING

Some ancient philosopher said that each man, to be
complete, must build a house, have a son, and write a book.

Writing is the toughest part. Our hectic lives don't give
us enough time to write – too many distractions exist.
The motivation is lacking; we fear the end result will
not be worth the effort.

And yet writing, for those who cannot paint a picture or
write music, is a basic form of expression. It is like painting
a landscape or writing a melody with words.

I think I'll keep writing with the full understanding that my
writing will not leave important footprints.

April 1986

ON A BLACK FRIEND

We made friends with a black man in Botswana named Berri. He is a man of middle age with a wonderful smiling face and with a real sense of pride in his work. Berri finds game and assists in the hunt.

Communication with this gentleman was difficult, and yet, with the exchange of a few words I knew he had a sense of humor, that he appreciated beauty, and that he had a real sense of compassion as well.

No doubt across the vast continent of Africa there are many, many people with these qualities. Sadly, there are not many smiles in Africa in the 1980s; the problems of politics, of AIDS, of starvation, or economic disaster are simply too immense.

There were empty moments on safari when I wished I could do more for Berri. It was perhaps easiest to accept his friendship for what it was.

Before leaving, Bayard gave Berri his safari hat. Clearly, this made him a happy man. It was a wonderfully random act of generosity.

August 1986

ON JW, Jr. – AS AN ORGANIZER

Jay's intensity is like a laser beam. His enthusiasm for
hunting generates a new approach, a new set of plans
each day. His consumption of history and government and
facts of all kinds is enormous and his storage capacity is
close to encyclopedic.

He seems to have had a grand time on safari, and this
may be the most important thing of all. We had some
high-quality time together.

All of us need to have a good time once in a while and
get away from the structured, value-established world
where we live.

The real challenge of the workplace is right around
the corner for Jay as I think about the final chapters
of my own life.

November 1986

ON THE MOON

One night I sat alone by the fire at our campsite in Botswana,
lost in thought. In time I shook the lonely feeling and walked
toward my tent to retire. The dry, flat landscape around
me was clearly visible, and looking directly above me
I discovered the moon was full.

Reaching for my binoculars and a chair, I sat down to focus
on the biggest, brightest, clearest moon I had ever seen.
The craters could not be identified through the powerful
binoculars, but the roughness of the terrain jumped across
the night sky which seemed so clear. After admiring this
dramatic view of the moon for a full five minutes, I asked
my companions if they would like to have a long look.

"I'm not into it," one of them replied. It made me think that
so many of the spectacles – or the music, the art, the sports,
the games, the joys for that matter – which I find special may
not seem so to those I am with. Such is life.

August 1986

ON DOGS

Dogs can provide a special brand of companionship to a young boy or an aging man, but it is difficult to focus on the relationship and nurture it properly during the middle years. It seems those are the years of production – of developing a profession and a specialty – but now that I am fifty and have a young son, it would be pleasant to bring another dog into the family. The idea appeals to Libby. (Perhaps she can take credit for the thought along with so many others.)

Ted and Lib and I will be on the lookout for a dog, although I suspect it will be quite some time before we get any four-legged creatures of any kind.

September 1986

ON MONEY

Money is a means of having a positive impact with one's life. It is nothing more. It shouldn't be hoarded, or stored, or counted. It should be managed properly.

Sadly, money throws a high voltage component into family arguments and it takes a psychiatrist to sort out the mess.

Perhaps Mr. Rockefeller – the one who made all the money – was right when he said he was doing his children a disservice by leaving them all his shekels.

In the final analysis, the important inheritance is everything we leave behind other than money.

October 1986

www.ingramcontent.com/pod-product-compliance
Lightning Source LLC
Chambersburg PA
CBHW070831100426
42813CB00003B/566